YOUR KNOWLEDGE HAS VALUE

- We will publish your bachelor's and master's thesis, essays and papers

- Your own eBook and book - sold worldwide in all relevant shops

- Earn money with each sale

Upload your text at www.GRIN.com
and publish for free

Bibliographic information published by the German National Library:

The German National Library lists this publication in the National Bibliography; detailed bibliographic data are available on the Internet at http://dnb.dnb.de .

This book is copyright material and must not be copied, reproduced, transferred, distributed, leased, licensed or publicly performed or used in any way except as specifically permitted in writing by the publishers, as allowed under the terms and conditions under which it was purchased or as strictly permitted by applicable copyright law. Any unauthorized distribution or use of this text may be a direct infringement of the author s and publisher s rights and those responsible may be liable in law accordingly.

Imprint:

Copyright © 2018 GRIN Verlag
Print and binding: Books on Demand GmbH, Norderstedt Germany
ISBN: 9783668645820

This book at GRIN:

https://www.grin.com/document/413987

John Tuttle

What Marijuana, "The Lord of the Rings", and Jazz Music Have in Common

A Look at the American Pop Culture and Counterculture of the 1960's

GRIN Verlag

GRIN - Your knowledge has value

Since its foundation in 1998, GRIN has specialized in publishing academic texts by students, college teachers and other academics as e-book and printed book. The website www.grin.com is an ideal platform for presenting term papers, final papers, scientific essays, dissertations and specialist books.

Visit us on the internet:

http://www.grin.com/

http://www.facebook.com/grincom

http://www.twitter.com/grin_com

What Marijuana, The Lord of the Rings, and Jazz Music Have in Common - A Look at the American Pop Culture and Counterculture of the 1960's

by John Tuttle

Preface

Three main themes recur throughout this text, saturating nearly every point of our discussion: news, society, and (obviously enough) culture. News affects society, thereby affecting culture which in turn affects the news, the society, and the culture itself. This is a relevant fact present throughout the whole history of the United States. Harriet Beecher Stowe's novel *Uncle Tom's Cabin* (1852) was an influential piece of anti-slavery pop culture, and the tragic tale it told changed the hearts and minds of many American whites in regards to their views on slavery.

Another prime example of how what makes the headlines also forms our pop culture can be found in the creation of the film monster Godzilla. In World War II, the U.S. released two atomic bombs on Japan, killing millions of innocent people. Naturally, Japan viewed atomic tests in a very negative light for years to follow. The 1954 Japanese sci-fi film *Godzilla* dramatically depicts the horrors that result from radioactive testing. These are just a few instances which show what an impact man's actions can have on society and culture and vice versa.

As anyone can attest to, Charles Darwin's book *On the Origin of Species* (1859) and his theory of evolution without the assistance of a Supreme Intellect have changed the scientific way in which we think about animals and about ourselves. Whether this was a change for the better (as many believe in regards to the fields of science) or for worse, a dramatic change it truly was. And not too many years after it seemed to have shed light in the society of science, Darwinism was applied to economic practices in late 19th century America.

Now known as "social Darwinism," this was a practice of employing Darwinian terminology and concepts in the realms of society, politics, and most importantly the economy. Among the businessmen and academics of the day, there were numbers of which fully accepted and promoted the usage of such ideologies in society. Capitalism and racism were often adopted by quite a few of the Social Darwinists. American Social Darwinists, such as William Graham Sumner, stated they believed that a nation's existence relied on unchecked economic competition.

They wanted no government interference. Only the strong would survive; that was the summary of their designs. They did not believe in charity or assisting the monetarily poor. However, some did consider particular races superior to others. (Adolf Hitler would develop similar beliefs just a few decades later.) Many political theorists of the time, using the Darwinian theory to aid in their own theorizing, attempted to make the point that poverty was, in fact, the product of natural inferiority. This train of thought inspired eugenics which continued into the 1970's.

Thus, we can say that Darwinism has affected society and culture and therefore the news. And most importantly it has become part of history. Countless more exemplars appear throughout the timelines of the world. But perhaps more so than in any other era in modern history, the 1960's was a rather turbulent decade full of drastic alterations in culture as well as society, particularly in America.

An Overview of the 1960's

The sixties, like any decade in modern history, was undergoing changes in nearly every aspect of life and thought. It was a brand new and revolutionary age in the development of film, music, and literature, and every form of entertainment. The United States in the 1960's introduced new cultural and scientific concepts to the general public.

In 1961, the famed Russian cosmonaut Yuri Gagarin became the first human being to travel into outer space, only to meet with a violent accident seven years later when he and a flight instructor were killed in a jet fighter crash. In 1969, near the close of this boiling and brimming decade, the American astronauts Neil Armstrong and Edwin "Buzz" Aldrin made history when they became the first Earthlings to touch down and walk on the surface of another celestial body, our Moon.

In spite of humanity's magnificent ingenuity and daring during that period, the sixties was also a time filled with turmoil, uprising, disagreement, and breakouts of violence. This was especially prevalent in regards to racial and sexual equality and liberty. On February 1, 1960, four black college students sat at a counter (designated strictly for white customers) in a store in Greensboro, North Carolina, refusing to budge. The "sit-in" strategy they displayed inspired many other such incidents throughout the Southern states.

In 1961, "freedom rides," were coordinated and carried out on buses going from the District of Columbia to New Orleans. As noted in Mary Jane Capozzoli Ingui's *American History, 1877 to the Present*, "Blacks and whites challenged the segregation of buses, rest rooms, and restaurants, and violence often erupted" (Ingui 168). The "freedom summer" of 1964 was another large movement with bearing to racial differences; it was a huge voter registration promotion in the South. Three of the movement's volunteers disappeared from Philadelphia, Mississippi in June. Later it was learned that they had been murdered by Ku Klux Klan members.

Riots exploded in approximately 75 cities in the U.S. between 1967 and 1968. These are said to be the reaction provoked by white control over business and property, unemployment, poverty, and police brutality. (In the sixties the fuzz, the heat, the man, and other terms became common synonyms for policemen or the police force.) Dr. Martin Luther King, Jr.'s assassination in Memphis, Tennessee in 1968 fueled rioting in over three dozen cities alone.

This was not the only devastating assassination in America which was hosted in the 1960's. Unfortunately, there were a number of others which require mentioning. John F. Kennedy, the first Catholic president of the United States (and a proponent of the space race), was fatally shot in Dallas, Texas in 1963. JFK was the fourth president to have been assassinated. His alleged killer, Lee Harvey Oswald, was also shot at a later time. His brother, Robert F. Kennedy, was also shot and killed in 1968, the same year that Martin Luther King was assassinated.

In the midst of this, one of the most memorable movements of history sprouted and flowered: the counterculture, otherwise known as the Hippie Movement. Making a big scene out of things, hippies emerged in the early 1960's and associated themselves with drug use, long hair, and permissive sexuality. Marijuana, as will be discussed in a bit more detail, was not the only drug used by the counterculture. The other big one that we know about is LSD.

Psychology professor Timothy Leary was a strong promoter of the use of psychedelic drugs in the sixties. He experimented with psilocybin, a compound found in certain varieties of fungi, in relation to its effects on human behavior. Leary went so far as to test this drug on inmates and seminary students! Then he started to use LSD in the early 1960's, believing that LSD was the supreme answer to decrease or eliminate psychic pain. Among the common possible effects caused by LSD are hallucinations, distorted sense of time, and impulsive behavior.

The Pot Culture

Marijuana (otherwise known as black gunion, African black, giggle weed, reefer, grass, yellow submarine, Mary Jane, pot, etc., etc.) has obviously had a great influence on human behavior and human actions due to its use down through the centuries. It made a big impact on popular culture and the general public's consideration when the movie *Reefer Madness* came out in 1936. It inaccurately depicts college students becoming prone to murder and suicide after smoking or consuming marijuana.

Reefer Madness is still shown on college campuses and theaters which specialize in art films. However, the old movie relies on a fantastical falsehood. In reality, pot does not turn people into crazed animals intent on violently killing people. In fact, it does quite the opposite for most who ingest it. Noticeable effects include red eyes, dry mouth, dizziness, increased hunger, and especially slow reaction time (meaning individuals doped up on marijuana tend to be nonviolent and dazed.)

Marijuana had its first influence on the counterculture which would thrive in the 1960's in the previous decade. During the 1950's, what is known as the Beat Movement (also referred to as the Beat Generation) was begun. The "Beats" wrote poetry and smoked pot; it's as simple as that. And many struggled to become published writers. When the counterculture of the sixties came about, the hippies were inspired by the Beat poets, their works, and even their lifestyle. Thus, marijuana was "at the center of the counterculture movement" (Collins 22).

College campuses have long hosted the saplings of change. There are countless groups, movements, and strikes which have begun at colleges and have spread across the continent and across the globe. The youth going through higher education are the minds that shape the future. So it is today; so it was also in the sixties. It was in that psychedelic decade that college students rebelled and transformed into hippies.

The Beat, the Jazz, and the Blues

What we know today as the beat music genre has little or nothing to do with the Beat Generation of the fifties and early sixties. To stay on topic, I will be primarily discussing the movement and not the music. The Beats (or Beatniks) consisted of American writers and other various artists who did drugs, listened to jazz music, and tended to reject materialism. (These creatives claimed their use of drugs was to see what artistic styles they could generate while they were high.)

Among the most well known of the Beats are Jack and Joan Kerouac, Allen Ginsberg, William S. Burroughs, and Neal and Carolyn Cassady. These and others of the Beat Generation heavily influenced the Hippie Movement of the sixties and seventies. Believe it or not, much of the terminology which surfaced in the 1960's had its roots in popular music from the past.

For example, the slang word "truckin'" came to us out of old American blues, particularly Blind Boy Fuller's 1930's song "Truckin' My Blues Away." Truckin' was used a lot in the sixties and seventies under the definition of "strutting with a specific goal in mind." Cat, as in "a cool dude," originated from jazz lingo. "Cat" was a term often applied to a jazz musician, and in the 1960's it was brought to new life as it became a familiar expression used by the everyday youth, including hippies.

Many other phrases employed fluently throughout the sixties such as "square," "threads," "far out," "it's a gas," and "hip" had their beginnings in jazz lingo. Hip was a term that even found its way into the book *On the Road* (1957) by Jack Kerouac of the Beat Generation. This book became a hot piece of pop culture for an entire generation of Americans in the sixties.

Bogart, after the Hollywood actor Humphrey Bogart, was transformed into a unique term. Humphrey Bogart was constantly seen smoking on the big screen. Thus, it is not too surprising that, in 1968, the song "Don't Bogart Me" was released. The newly coined term "bogarting" meant "keeping to oneself." The revolutionary song gained more fame with its use in the counterculture film of the following year, *Easy Rider*, directed by Dennis Hopper.

Tolkien and The Lord of the Rings

J.R.R. Tolkien was the genius behind the creation of the novel *The Hobbit* and the fantasy trilogy *The Lord of the Rings* which was first published in the 1950's in the United Kingdom. Tolkien was a man of passions and talents as well as one who often enjoyed a pint at a pub and a puff from his pipe. A very learned individual, the Oxford professor was dedicated to his work which involved perhaps his fondest love: literature. He was an avid reader and, of course, a splendid writer. He simply loved writing; he did not care whether it was ever published or not.

A poet, critic, translator, editor, teacher, and author, Tolkien was among the sagest literary giants of his day, and he is still considered in high esteem in present times. He corresponded with friends through his letters; he wrote stories to entertain his children; he spent hours making maps, illustrations, and alphabets associated with his chief work which was the tales of Middle-earth.

Many of Tolkien's characters are fond of some of the same favorite pastimes such as writing, smoking, and drinking. Everybody in Middle-earth smokes and drinks, but many of the hobbits are the ones who are shown to be extremely literate. If you know the classic tale, you are aware that several of the main hobbits such as Bilbo and Frodo are writers. And, as accurately depicted in the films, hobbits like smoking their "pipeweed."

In the prologue to the first novel installment of *The Lord of the Rings*, Tolkien states this of the hobbits:

"'The Bree-hobbits claim to have been the first actual smokers of the pipe-weed... And certainly it was from Bree that the art of smoking the genuine **weed** spread in the recent centuries among Dwarves and such other folk, Rangers, Wizards, or wanderers, as still passed to and fro through that ancient road-meeting'" (*The Fellowship of the Ring* 29).

The Baggins family, that hobbit clan to which both Bilbo and Frodo belong, live in a peaceful place called the Shire where people have little or no worries. The Shire is also home to a number of inns which host not only room and board but also provide haunts for the locals to congregate and drink ale. One such inn just happens to be called the **Green Dragon**.

The phrases in bold are bold for a reason. They were not extraordinary in Tolkien's world nor to Tolkien himself. For instance, when he writes "weed" he is talking about a made-up plant which is grown and smoked by hobbits. But these were words which the hippies of the counterculture probably would have been familiar with. Weed, as we know, refers to marijuana. Green Dragon is actually the name of an alcoholic beverage which has had marijuana soaked in it for a period of time.

These are not the only things the hippies and hobbits had in common. As the nonfiction book *The Hobbit Party* somewhat comically states, "The hobbits, after all, were even into mushrooms, for goodness' sake" (Richards and Witt 39). *The Hobbit Party* also divulges the fact that *The Lord of the Rings* was not released by an American publisher until the 1960's and that in the same decade the novels sold like hotcakes on college campuses.

A great number of those college consumers consisted of hippies. Thus, many hippies were likely influenced by this epic piece of pop culture. Since the hobbits were heroes in *The Lord of the Rings*, an impressionable individual could consider everything the hobbits did to be glamorous and heroic. If so, such an individual might believe drinking and smoking were honorable actions which made life better when, in fact, they simply do not. Hobbits, since small in stature, were often brushed off by larger folk who deemed them of having little strength or merit. This could have made them even more relatable to hippies.

Even such renowned American figures as actor Leonard Nimoy (Spock in *Star Trek*) helped contribute to the hype of this mounting fad. The Hollywood actor did this, whether intentionally or not, when he was featured in the 1967 *Malibu U* music video, "The Ballad of Bilbo Baggins," which can easily put its viewers in good humor. He recalled in an interview that he quite enjoyed the hobbit stories. This goofy ditty also appeared on Nimoy's album entitled *Highly Illogical*.

Well-known literary figures of the sixties, such as the American sci-fi and fantasy author Lin Carter, responded rapidly to the American frenzy over the Middle-earth trilogy with critical and analytical books discussing *The Lord of the Rings*, its meaning, and the effects it was having in the United States. Tolkien's renowned trilogy was published in America in 1965. By 1969, Carter had written and had published his review and analysis, entitled *Tolkien: A Look Behind the Lord of the Rings*. And other critical looks at Tolkien and his story's background, such as William Ready's *Understanding Tolkien and The Lord of the Rings*, were published in relatively the same period.

Sci-fi author Lin Carter, for one, jokingly claimed that sci-fi readers of America were the first to discover the tales of Middle-earth, also saying, "As is well known, science fiction fans read that crazy rocketship stuff; if they can swallow that, they can take anything" (*Tolkien: A Look Behind the Lord of the Rings* 1). He also made the point of the observation that numerous American fanzines quickly sprouted up in response to the renewed success of *The Lord of the Rings*. One of the fan magazines was even called **Green Dragon**.

It is a historical fact that J.R.R. Tolkien himself considered his American popularity a strange thing as recounted in another critical review from the sixties, "His [Tolkien's] fame in America is a puzzle to him, although it pleases, perplexes and bothers him. It's a tangent from his real purpose as a writer" (Ready 18).

Despite its association with the drastic counterculture, certain critics have actually considered the epic masterpiece (a title to which it has some right to have bestowed upon it) to be the greatest fictional work of the 20th century. It definitely inspired and influenced many works of fantasy that would be written for years afterward. But there was more going on in the realms of pop culture and entertainment during that decade that made *The Lord of the Rings* stand out.

Science Fiction and Entertainment in the 1960's

The 1960's produced an explosion of fantasy and sci-fi entertainment. Meanwhile, the very face of science fiction was being reshaped. Lin Carter was just one of the novelists who used sci-fi to their advantage. Others include Walter M. Miller, Anthony Burgess, and James Joyce. Robert A. Heinlein was also a key literary figure. A science fiction author, he is best known for *Stranger in a Strange Land* (1961).

This novel was practically a holy code for the counterculture. It ended up "inspiring not just secular polygamous communes but also the Church of All Worlds, a still-flourishing New Age sect incorporated in 1968" (Jeet Heer). Heinlein was said to have led a complex "and contradictory life." The man's works were also riddled with countless other biased political references, some of which looked favorably upon by libertarians and authoritarians.

The science fiction of the 1960's is, I suppose, classical when looked back on from a modern perspective, yet the sci-fi/fantasy of that era is not as classical as the works of H.G. Wells, Jules Verne, and C.S. Lewis (the last of whom was a contemporary of J.R.R. Tolkien). What differentiated the separate eras? It was simply the content. The sixties' authors introduced literature which was laced with what had previously been considered rather taboo subjects including sex, politics, and religion.

This could have been what made *The Lord of the Rings* really pop in American pop culture during the 1960's. Though loved by sci-fi fans, it was really a work of pure fantasy. And, unlike the literature written in the sixties, Tolkien's work did not touch on the topics of religion or sex, though many of the morals of his story were based on the Catholic faith. And despite the fact that some of Tolkien's political/economic views shine through in his writing, the author does not go off on a tirade on such points.

In short, Tolkien's masterpiece was of an older age, the product of decades of work and thinking out a plot, whereas the sixties science fiction was a bit more shallow. Thus, *The Lord of the Rings* could have appealed to a much wider audience than the fictional literature of the day.

As previously noted, the sixties, like the decade in which we live now, was filled with racial unrest, particularly regarding African Americans. It was this decade that gave rise to several new Marvel superheroes such as Thor and even Black Panther and the Falcon. Black Panther, created by Stan Lee, is considered the first black superhero to appear in mainstream American comics. His character first appeared in 1966. Coincidentally, the Black Panther Party, a militant political party founded by Huey Newton, was begun the very same year. Some people even misassociated the political party with the comic book character.

At the same time when these new superheroes were emerging in comics, older superheroes like Batman and the Green Hornet got their own TV programs. The 1960's was not only a golden era of science fiction; it was a golden era of television as well. Many sci-fi series, Westerns, and household or family-orientated sitcoms thrived during this period not to mention Rod Serling's *The Twilight Zone* series which included concepts such as humanity, existence, aliens, dystopias, and apocalypses and which lies in a genre in and of itself.

Hollywood film director/producer Irwin Allen created four individual sci-fi TV series during the 1960's. But perhaps the most enduring and memorable of the sci-fi shows of the sixties was *Star Trek* which competed with Allen's *Lost in Space*. Like the thrilled readers of *The Lord of the Rings*, avid followers of *Star Trek* generated fanzines very soon after the show's initial success, the first being *Spockanalia* which was in print by 1967. Many shows in the sixties made note of the counterculture movement. *Star Trek* and the comedic *Batman* showcased it as did *Lost in Space*, *Get Smart*, and *Mister Ed*.

Film was also undergoing an evolution. More and more films were focusing on special effects, and this made for some stunning science fiction entertainment. Eight different *Godzilla* films were filmed and released during the decade. (Currently, this marks the most amount of *Godzilla* movies to be made in a ten-year period.) In fact, the sixties even produced two of the longest remembered science fiction films of all time, both of which were released to theaters in 1968.

The sixties brought a large interest in space travel as well as chimps, surprisingly enough. In 1961, an ape named Ham became the first chimpanzee to fly in space. (Monkeys had been used in a previous flight.) After Darwin's *On the Origin of Species* was published in 1859, the primary debate it caused in the scientific community was concerning the similarities or differences between human beings and apes. Several scientific developments and newly proposed hypotheses in the 1960's shed new light on biochemistry and the theory of evolution.

At the same time, Jane Goodall was studying chimpanzees in the African country of Tanzania. Unlike what was generally believed about chimps and other apes, Goodall discovered they were intelligent and seemingly emotional creatures capable of making and using simple tools. Her findings were publicized via a 1965 TV program from National Geographic.

What better time for popular culture to use apes and the concept of evolution to its advantage? And so it did. But not initially in America. It actually came out of France originally. Pierre Boulle's 1963 novel, *La Planète des Singes*, translated into English as *Planet of the Apes*, was very quickly picked up by the filmmakers in Hollywood. The first *Planet of the Apes* film was released in 1968; it starred Charleton Heston and (since sex was overemphasized in the sixties) showed blatant male nudity. Ever since then, the *Planet of the Apes* saga has consisted of a number of films, novels, comics, and even a TV series (1974).

The other sci-fi cult classic which appeared on the big screen in 1968 was *2001: A Space Odyssey* which, like *Planet of the Apes*, employed masterfully crafted ape suits for the performers. (In *2001*, apes are depicted in the beginning of the film on earth and come in contact with a monolith.) A very bizarre yet stunningly well filmed and well edited work, *2001* was, once again like *Planet of the Apes*, based on a novel: Arthur C. Clarke's *2001: A Space Odyssey*, originally published in 1968. This original sci-fi novel and its contemporary film of the same title sparked three more novels in the franchise written by Clarke and another film, *2010: The Year We Make Contact*.

Conclusion

The 1960's is an ample exemplar of how pop culture such as literature and music from the past can shape modern society through affecting people's knowledge, understanding, vocabulary, recreation, and life decisions. Whether for better or for worse, popular culture always has and always will have a significant bearing on humanity's actions and behavior.

Traditional Sources:

Carter, Lin. *Tolkien: A Look Behind "The Lord of the Rings"*. Ballantine Books, 1969.

Collins, Anna. *Marijuana: Abuse and Legalization*. Lucent Press, 2017.

Horobin, Wendy, et al., editors. *Space: A Visual Encyclopedia*. DK Publishing, 2010.

Ingui, Mary Jane Capozzoli. *American History, 1877 to the Present*. Barron's Educational Series, Inc., 2003.

Marlowe, Lynn. *CLEP History of the United States II: 1865 to the Present*. Research & Education Association, Inc., 2013.

Ready, William. *Understanding Tolkien and The Lord of the Rings*. Henry Regnery Company, 1968.

Thorne, Ian. *Godzilla*. Crestwood House, Inc., 1982.

Tolkien, J. R. R. "Prologue." *The Fellowship of the Ring*, Ballantine Books, 1965, pp. 20–36.

Witt, Jonathan, and Jay W. Richards. *The Hobbit Party: The Vision of Freedom That Tolkien Got, and the West Forgot*. Ignatius Press, 2014.

Online Sources:

Baekgaard, Jakob. "The Word Is Beat: Jazz, Poetry & the Beat Generation." *All About Jazz*, 12 Aug. 2015, www.allaboutjazz.com/the-word-is-beat-jazz-poetry-and-the-beat-generation-by-jakob-baekgaard.php.

Gioia, Ted. "When Science Fiction Grew Up." *Conceptual Fiction*, 29 Sept. 2014, conceptualfiction.com/whenscifigrewup.html.

Heer, Jeet. "A Famous Science Fiction Writer's Descent Into Libertarian Madness." *New Republic*, 8 June 2014, newrepublic.com/article/118048/william-pattersons-robert-heinlein-biography-hagiography.

Jose, Maria, and John Tenuto. "Spockanalia -- The First Star Trek Fanzine." *StarTrek.com*, 20 Oct. 2014, www.startrek.com/article/spockanalia-the-first-star-trek-fanzine.

Kilkenny, Katie. "When Spock Sang about The Hobbit." *Slate*, 14 Dec. 2012, www.slate.com/blogs/browbeat/2012/12/14/ballad_of_bilbo_baggins_leonard_nimoy_aka_spock_sings_an_ode_to_tolkein.html.

Liptak, Andrew. "The Unauthorized Lord of the Rings." *Kirkus Reviews*, 5 Dec. 2013, www.kirkusreviews.com/features/unauthorized-lord-rings/.

MacLaren, Erik. "The Effects of Acid." *DrugAbuse.com*, 4 Apr. 2017, drugabuse.com/library/effects-acid-lsd/.

Sebesta, Robbe Lyn. "Timothy Leary and the 1960's Counter-Culture." *Catholic Stand*, 29 Oct. 2013, www.catholicstand.com/timothy-leary-and-the-1960s-counter-culture/.

"Bobby Kennedy Is Assassinated." *History.com*, A&E Television Networks, www.history.com/this-day-in-history/bobby-kennedy-is-assassinated.

"The Decision to Go to the Moon: President John F. Kennedy's May 25, 1961 Speech before a Joint Session of Congress." Edited by Steve Garber, NASA, 29 Oct. 2013, history.nasa.gov/moondec.html.

"Jane Goodall's Wild Chimpanzees." *PBS*, Public Broadcasting Service, 27 Oct. 2014, www.pbs.org/wnet/nature/jane-goodalls-wild-chimpanzees-jane-goodalls-story/1911/.

"Social Darwinism in the Gilded Age." *Khan Academy*, www.khanacademy.org/humanities/ap-us-history/period-6/apush-gilded-age/a/social-darwinism-in-the-gilded-age.

"Words of the 60s: Far Out!" *Dictionary.com*, Dictionary.com, 2017, www.dictionary.com/e/s/60s-words/#cool-or-squaresville.

YOUR KNOWLEDGE HAS VALUE

- We will publish your bachelor's and master's thesis, essays and papers

- Your own eBook and book - sold worldwide in all relevant shops

- Earn money with each sale

Upload your text at www.GRIN.com
and publish for free